ISBN: 978-0-9919183-0-0

For any additional information or to contact the publisher, visit

www.grantworksmedia.com, or send an email to grantworksmedia@gmail.com.

Table Of Contents

Table Of Contents

A Brief Important Introduction

You won't know anything, so read this.

1

Steps

So Here's The Deal...

How This Book Works

So Here's The Deal...

We Are Assuming Some Things About You

1. You are thinking of creating or acquiring an app.

2. You want to sell an app for an iOS device (iPods, iPads, etc.)

3. You want to set up your accounts for when you're ready to sell an app.

4. You don't really know where to start.

I'm Gonna Make This Easy

This guide will literally be step-by-step, holding your hand through it all. Big print, explanations, and many many pictures!

This Is For iOS!

Don't get me wrong, Mac, Safari, PC, Android, and whatever are great and all, but this is a guide for developing apps solely for iOS devices. (iPods, iPads, etc.)

Whether Or Not You Have An App, You Will Need This Book Eventually

If you don't have an app, *that's okay*. You will need to register as a Developer anyway. No matter what you are doing, or might think of doing, this book will help you with the registrations. If, however, you happen to have an app, then follow along, and this book will get you to actually publishing your app on the App Store.

It's A Tutorial

That's all this book is, a tutorial. If you are looking for an in-depth coding guide for Apps, you are in the wrong place. This book will go step-by-step with you, from knowing nothing, to finally finding the "Submit App to App Store" button.

This Is About Getting Your App Out There

This guide will only focus on the *development process*. Registrations, websites, submissions, requirements. As long as you have an App that is almost ready to be sold.

This Is From Personal Experience

The process needed to go though for submitting Apps is a labyrinth of vague, unhelpful buttons. I clicked the right buttons, so I am now passing that information on to you.

How This Book Works

Each Step Will Have:

1. A heading describing it

2. A short explanation

3. What to do

4. A screenshot

It's Step-By-Step

This will take you, each and every bit of the way. I will tell you which buttons to click, but if you get lost or redirected, I will include links at every step to put you back on course.

You Can Use This As A Reference Guide Too...

If you already did most of these steps, or just want to find out more, you can read each step's explanation for clarification. Say you forgot a step, or don't quite remember how to do something, just use this book as a reference guide.

Becoming A Developer

2

You need to become a Developer to do anything.

Steps

Why?

In order to publish any iOS apps whatsoever, you need to become a *developer*. Luckily, you can become a developer very easily by signing up with Apple, and paying a $99 yearly fee. This section will walk you through the steps to become a developer, and help you understand the significance of doing so.

The Apple Developer Website

https://developer.apple.com

The Apple Developer website contains links to the iOS, Mac, and Safari *Development Centers*. In this guide, we will only be using the iOS Development Center. Although if you ever want to create apps for Mac or Safari, the Apple Developer website will take you where you need to go.

From this page, start by clicking the **iOS Dev Center** button at the center of the page. This links you to the iOS Development Center.

Figure 2.1 The Apple Developer Homepage

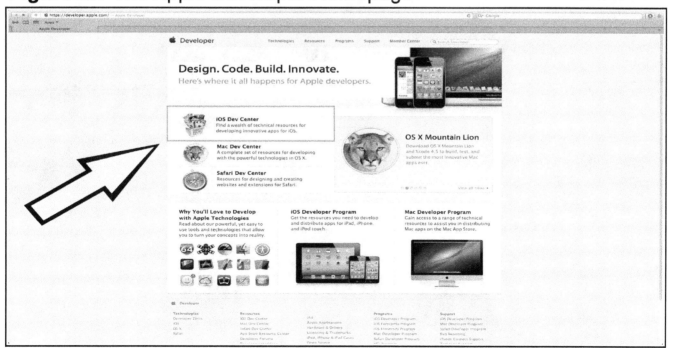

Find The iOS Development Center

https://developer.apple.com/devcenter/ios/index.action

This web page is where we will be most of the time. It contains downloads for the newest software such as Xcode, in-depth reference libraries, guides to help you, and the Certificates, Identifiers & Profiles site, which we will get into later.

Click the **Register** button at the top right hand side of the page.

Figure 2.2 The iOS Development Center Homepage

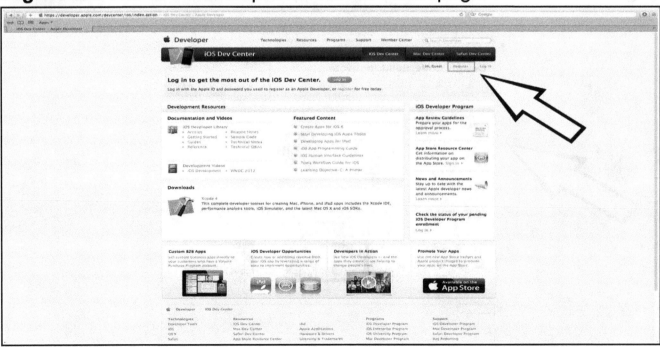

Registering As An Apple Developer

https://developer.apple.com/programs/register/

This is where you register. If you haven't created an Apple ID yet, you can do that here by clicking **Create Apple ID**. Otherwise, continue registering by clicking the **Sign in/Register** button right above.

Figure 2.3 The Developer Registration Page

Registered Apple Developer Resources

https://developer.apple.com/membercenter/index.action

Right now, from the iOS Development Center, If you click **Member Center** at the top of the page, you come here. Currently you have access to the *Registered Apple Developer Resources*, which aren't much.

This is not to be confused with the *Developer Program Resources*, which we will acquire in the next step.

Figure 2.4 Registered Apple Developer Resources

Enroll In The Developer Program

https://developer.apple.com/programs/ios/

To become an official developer, you must enroll in the iOS Developer Program. Navigate to the Apple Developer website (as seen on page 7), and then click on **iOS Developer Program** at the bottom of the page.

You will have to pay $99 (PayPal, credit card, etc), but afterwards, you will have access to all the privileges and bonuses an Apple developer gets.

Figure 2.5 Enroll In The Developer Program

Developer Program Resources

https://developer.apple.com/membercenter/index.action

You should now be an Apple developer. Having acquired the title, you have complete access to all the Developer Program Resources:

Certificates, Identifiers & Profiles allows you to manage your Profiles, Certificates, ID's etc.

iTunes Connect is where you will finally be submitting your app later.

App Store Resource Center, Apple Developer Forum, and Developer Support are all resources to help you answer your questions.

Figure 2.6 Developer Program Resources

Certificates, Identifiers & Profiles

Just to give you a general overview of it.

3

Steps

What's Happening...

1. Certificates Section

2. Identifiers Section

3. Devices Section

4. Provisioning Section

What's Happening...

https://developer.apple.com/account/overview.action

In this chapter, we will be covering the Certificates, Identifiers & Profiles section of the Apple Developer website. It is simply a quick place to access some certificates, ID's, and profiles. We will go through each tab and give a brief explanation of it, as we will go more in depth on them later.

Certificates Section

https://developer.apple.com/account/ios/certificate/certificateList.action

This section allows you to upload and manage your code signing certificates. We will be discussing this all in the next chapter so don't worry about it.

Figure 3.1 Certificates Section

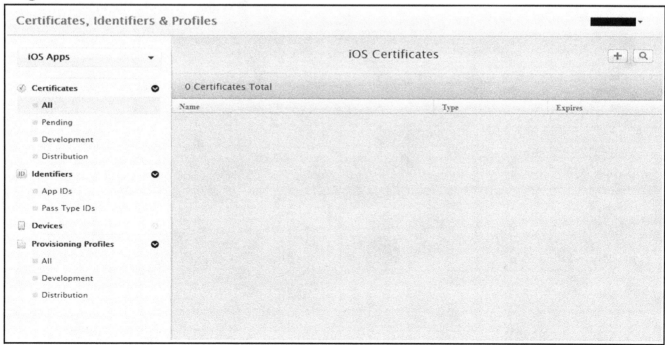

Identifiers Section

https://developer.apple.com/account/ios/identifiers/bundle/bundleList.action

Identifiers are what distinguish your app from every other app. It is a unique ID that will allow you to put your app on the App Store. We will create one later on.

Figure 3.2 Identifiers Section

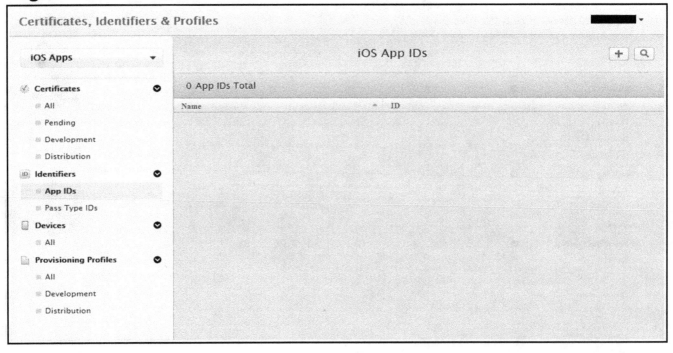

Devices Section

https://developer.apple.com/account/ios/device/deviceList.action

This section lets you manage the devices you will be using for your app development. You can have up to 100 different devices registered each year. We will walk through this later in the book.

Figure 3.3 Devices Section

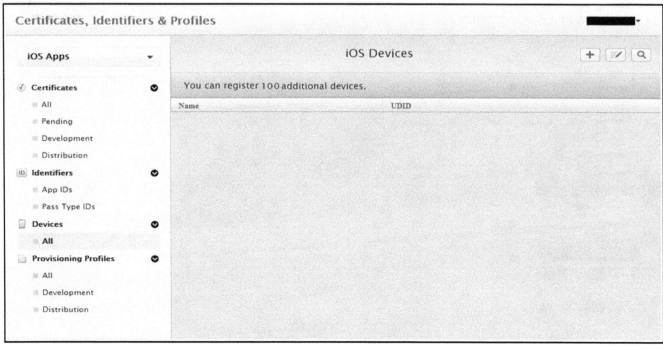

Provisioning Section

https://developer.apple.com/account/ios/profile/profileList.action

The Provisioning Profiles section allows you to create Provisioning Profiles. These pretty much let your app be tested on a device, and then, eventually sold. A Provisioning Profile must be installed on each device you wish to run your app's code. We will deal with this later in the book.

Figure 3.4 Provisioning Section

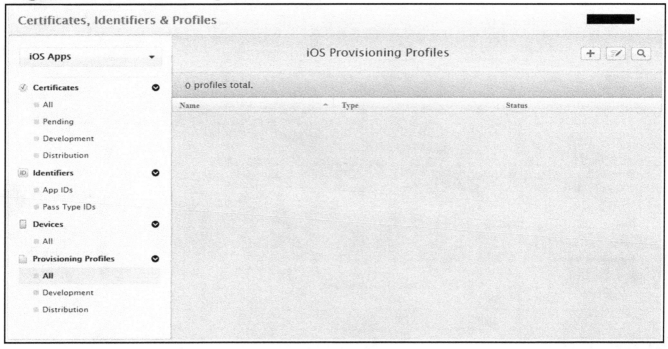

Requesting Your Certificates

We just have to *do* this. Don't ask why, just do it.

4

Oh God, What Is This?

Straight from the iOS Development Center:

"All iOS applications must be signed by a valid certificate before they can be run on an Apple device. In order to sign applications for testing purposes, Team Members need an iOS Development Certificate."

Essentially, we need to obtain some virtual "certificates", and "sign" our code with it. Luckily, you let Apple deal with signing your code. All you have to do is press a button.

Open Keychain Access

To manage our certificates, we have to find Keychain Access. On your Mac, Keychain Access is an application that can usually be accessed by going to:

Applications->Utilities->Keychain Access

Or if you have a later OSX, you can go to:

Launchpad->Utilities->Keychain Access

Figure 4.1 Open Keychain Access

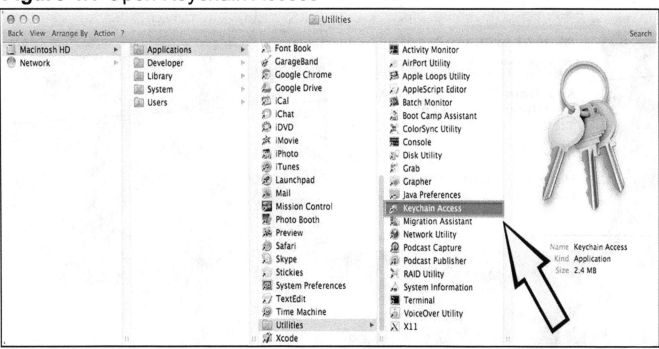

Keychain Preferences

With Keychain Access open, in the menu bar go to:

Keychain Access->Preferences

Figure 4.2 Keychain Preferences

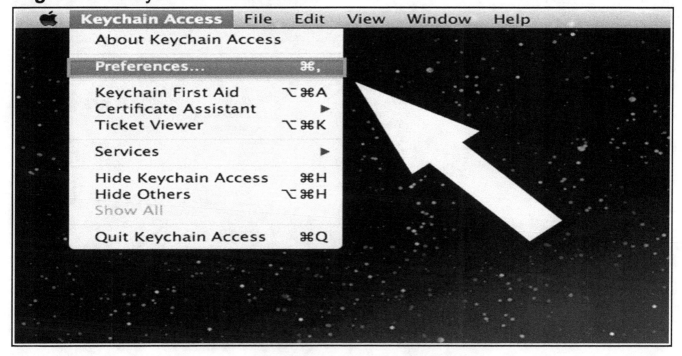

Certificates Tab

From the preferences menu, go to the *Certificates* tab and make sure that *Online Certificate Status Protocol (OCSP)* and *Certificate Revocation List (CRL)* are both set to **Off**.

Figure 4.3 Certificates Tab

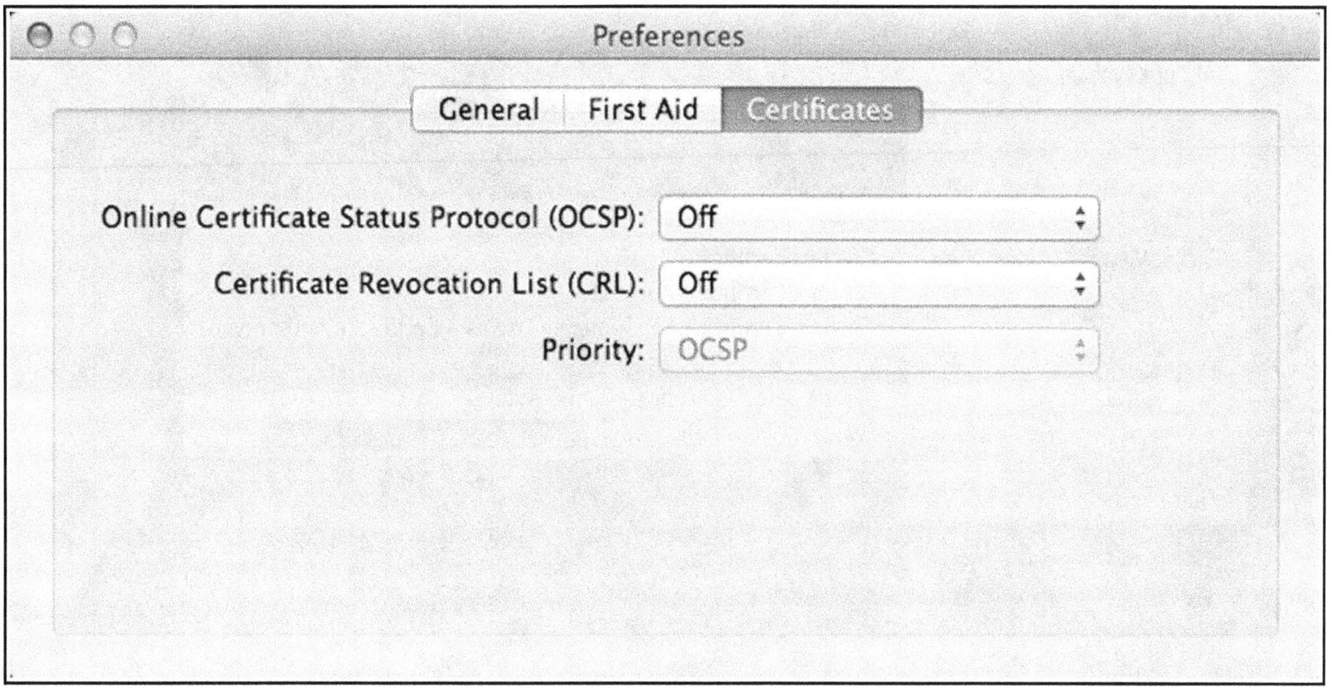

Open Certificate Assistant

Still with Keychain Access open, in the menu bar, now go to:

Keychain Access->Certificate Assistant->Request a Certificate From a Certificate Authority

Figure 4.4 Open Certificate Assistant

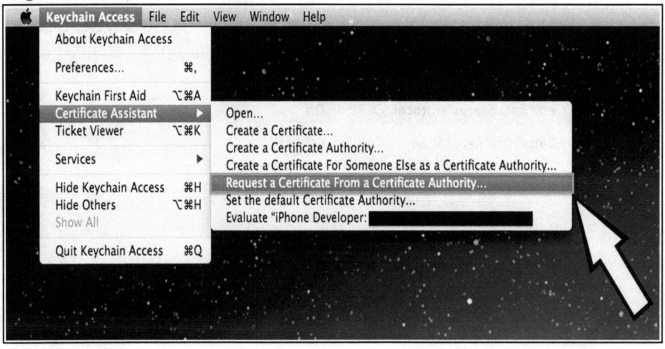

Certificate Information

With Certificate Assistant Open, fill in the boxes accordingly:

User Email Address: Put in the email address you used when you first signed up to be a developer.

Common Name: Fill in your first and last name.

Request is: Set to *Saved to Disk*, and check *Let me specify key pair information*.

Click **Continue**.

Figure 4.5 Certificate Information

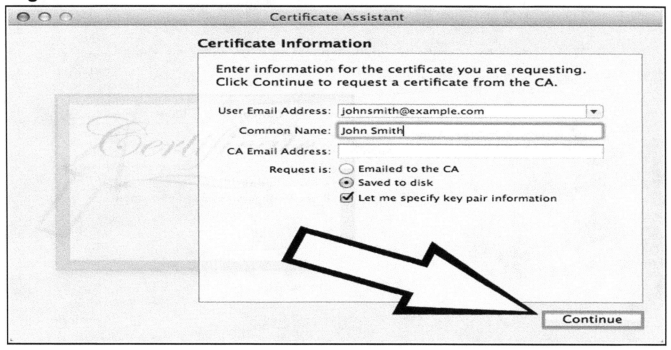

Save Your Certificate Request

With your information filled out, save your certificate request somewhere you will remember, as you will be needing it later.

Figure 4.6 Save Your Certificate Request

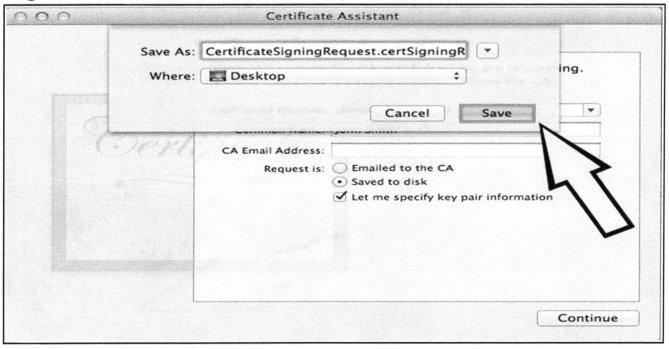

Key Pair Information

Save your key to somewhere you will remember, and then make sure the settings are as follows:

Key Size: Set to *2048 bits*.

Algorithm: Set to *RSA*.

Figure 4.7 Key Pair Information

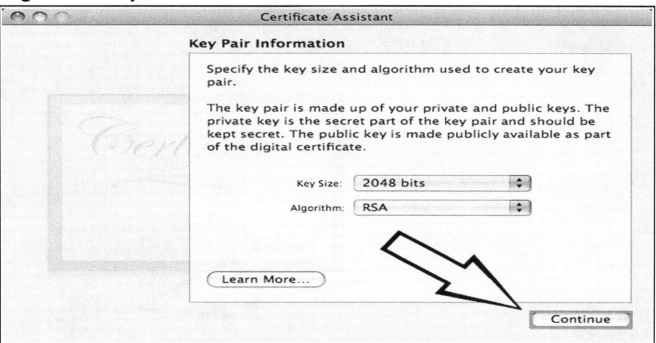

Your Request Is Created!

Having followed the above steps correctly, your certificate request should have been created at the location you specified.

Figure 4.8 Your Request Is Created!

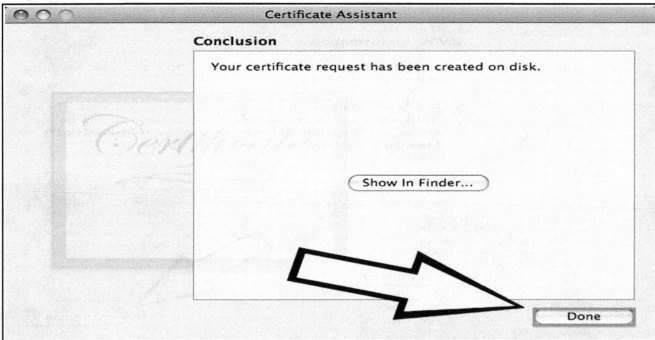

You Can See The Key

Your key request is completed and you can view or access the newly created key in Keychain Access under *Keychains* in the *login* section.

Figure 4.9 You Can See The Key

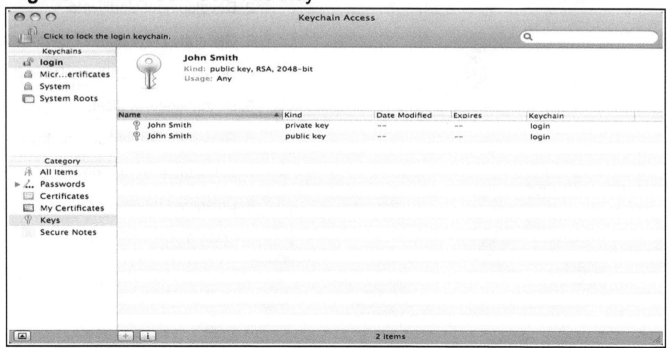

Uploading Your Certificates

It's *almost* done, just a few more steps!

5

I Thought We Just Did This...

In the last chapter we acquired a request for a certificate. Now, we have to upload that certificate request to their website, in order to activate it.

Certificates Section

https://developer.apple.com/ios/manage/certificates/team/index.action

In Certificates, Identifiers & Profiles, go to the Certificates section and navigate to any tab.

From here, click on the **+** sign in the top right corner of the page.

Figure 5.1 Certificates Section

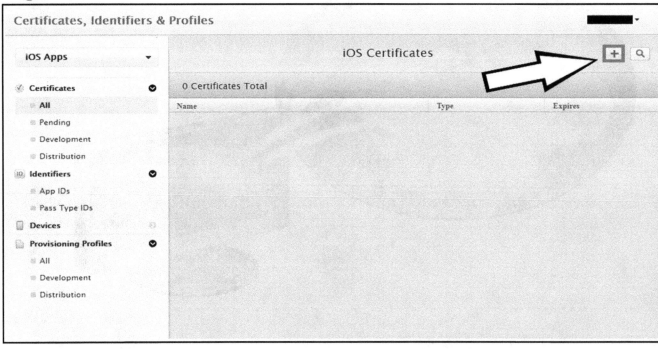

Development Certificate

Underneath *Development* heading, select **iOS App Development**. This will allow you to create a development certificate.

Click **Continue** at the bottom of the page.

Figure 5.2 Request Development Certificate

Development

◉ **iOS App Development**

Sign development versions of your iOS app.

◯ **Apple Push Notification service SSL (Sandbox)**

Establish connectivity between your notification server and the Apple Push Notification service sandbox environment. A separate certificate is required for each app you develop.

Generate Development Certificate

Once you've clicked through, you should end up at this page. Near the bottom of the page, click the **Choose File** button. Go to the location you previously saved your certificate request to, and select the file. The file's name should be:

CertificateSigningRequest.certSigningRequest

Figure 5.3 Select Certificate File

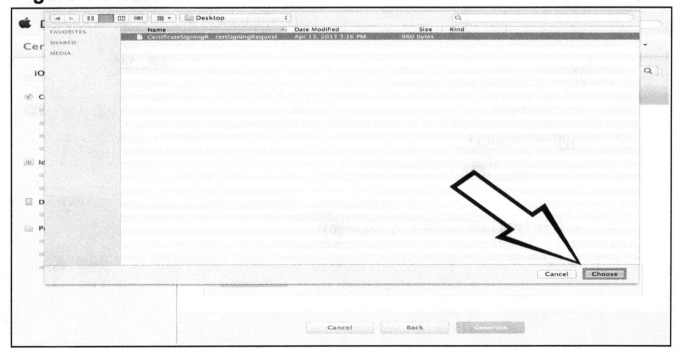

Development Certificate Issued!

Within a few short moments, this screen should appear. Your development certificate will have been issued, and can be downloaded now.

Click the blue **Download** button in the middle of the page.

Once you have saved the certificate to a place, click **Add Another** at the bottom of the page.

Figure 5.4 Your Certificate Is Ready

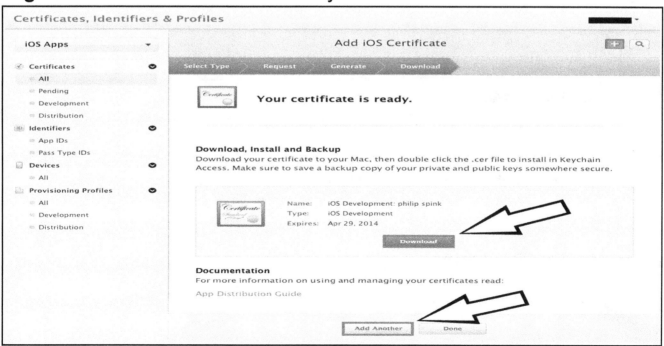

Distribution Certificate

Underneath *Distribution* heading, select **App Store and Ad Hoc**. This will allow you to create a distribution certificate.

Click **Continue** at the bottom of the page.

Figure 5.5 Request Distribution Certificate

Distribution

◉ **App Store and Ad Hoc**
Sign your iOS app for submission to the App Store or for Ad Hoc distribution.

○ **Apple Push Notification service SSL (Production)**
Establish connectivity between your notification server and the Apple Push Notification service production environment. A separate certificate is required for each app you distribute.

○ **Pass Type ID Certificate**
Sign and send updates to passes in Passbook.

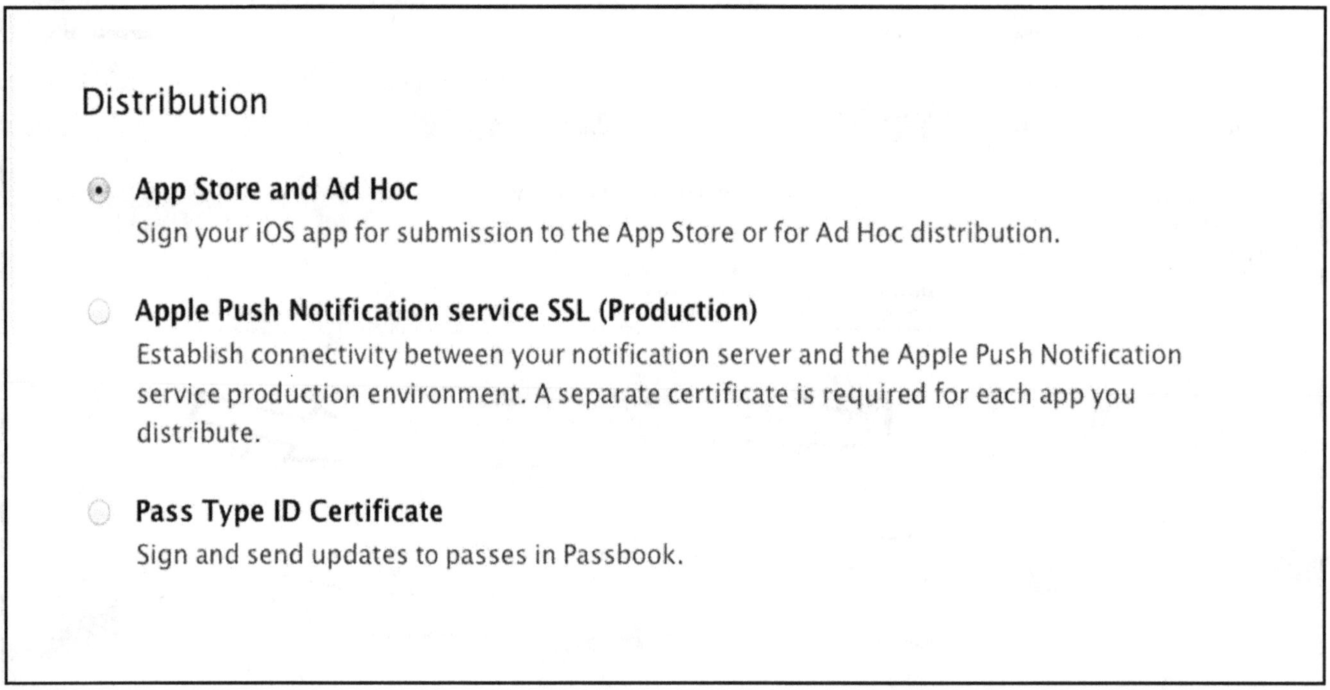

Generate Distribution Certificate

Once you've clicked through, you should end up at this page. Near the bottom of the page, click the **Choose File** button. Go to the location you previously saved your certificate request to, and select the file. The file's name should be:

CertificateSigningRequest.certSigningRequest

Figure 5.6 Select Certificate File

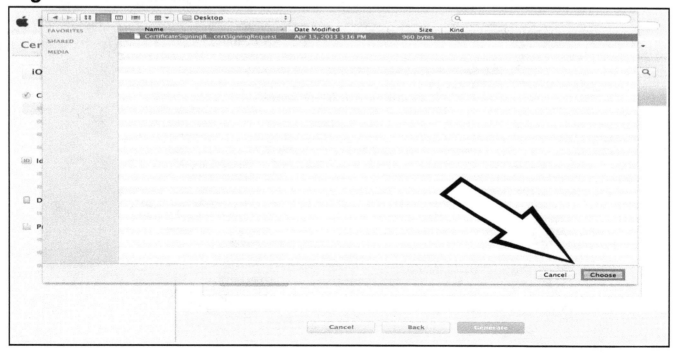

Distribution Certificate Issued!

Within a few short moments, this screen should appear. Your distribution certificate will have been issued, and can be downloaded now.

Click the blue **Download** button in the middle of the page.

Once you have saved the certificate to a place, click **Add Another** at the bottom of the page.

Figure 5.7 Your Certificate Is Ready

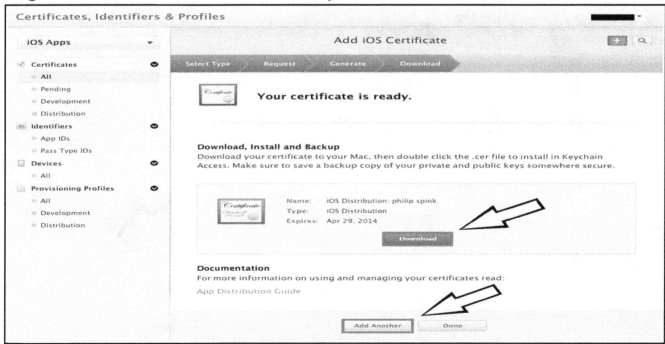

Download Intermediate Certificate

You should be back at the place where you can choose between development and distribution certificates. At the bottom of the page, there is a paragraph detailing *Intermediate Certificates*:

"To use your certificates, you must have the intermediate signing certificate in your system keychain. This is automatically installed by Xcode. However, if you need to reinstall the intermediate signing certificate click the link below:"

You should already have this certificate installed, but just in case, click the blue link underneath to download the certificate.

Figure 5.8 Download Your Certificates

Intermediate Certificates

To use your certificates, you must have the intermediate signing certificate in your system keychain. This is automatically installed by Xcode. However, if you need to reinstall the intermediate signing certificate click the link below:

Worldwide Developer Relations Certificate Authority

Apply Your Certificates

Re-open Keychain Access, and select the *Certificates* section on the left. Then, simply drag the three certificates you downloaded, individually into the box.

At first you may see a red warning under the certificate's information, but it will soon go away and be replaced with a green check mark followed by:

This certificate is valid.

Figure 5.9 Apply Your Certificates

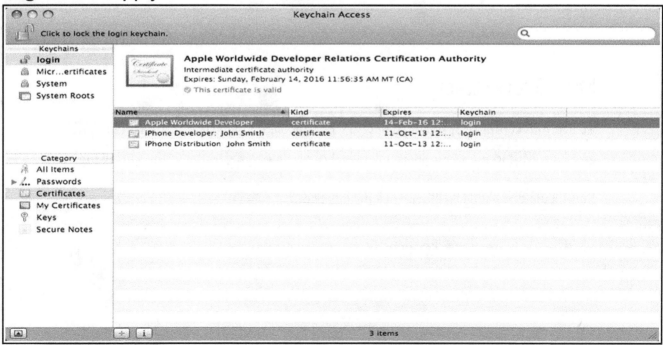

Adding A New Device

To test your app, you need to run it on a device.

I'm Starting To Get This...

In this chapter we will cover the Devices section of Certificates, Identifiers & Profiles. The main purpose of this is to register your Apple devices so that you can eventually use them to develop your app, using them to debug and test. In a chapter to come we will set up Provisioning Profiles, which will allow you to actually use your device for these purposes. You can have up to 100 devices registered at a time.

Devices Section

From Certificates, Identifiers, and Profiles, navigate your way to the Devices section. This is where you can register your devices for development purposes, like testing your app.

From here, click on the **+** sign in the top right corner of the page.

Figure 6.1 Devices Section

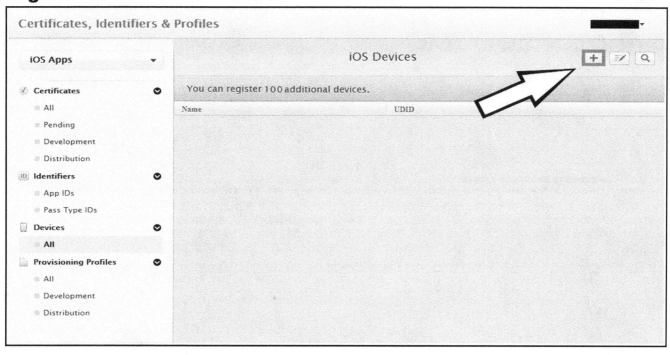

Add iOS Devices

After clicking the **+**, you should be here. This is where you enter the information pertaining to your device. You will have to enter a name, ex. "John's iPod", as well as your device's 40 digit UDID number.

In the next steps, we will show you how to acquire that 40 digit number.

Figure 6.2 Adding Devices

◉ **Register Device**
Name your device and enter its Unique Device Identifier (UDID).

Name: |

UDID:

○ **Register Multiple Devices**
Upload a file containing the devices you wish to register. Please note that a maximum of 100 devices can be included in your file and it may take a few minutes to process.
Download sample files

Choose File...

Cancel   Continue

Xcode Organizer

One way to get your device's 40 digit ID, is to plug it into your computer and then open Xcode (an application built into every Mac). From there, navigate to the organizer, and click on your device. Next to *Identifier* will be your number.

Figure 6.3 Xcode Organizer

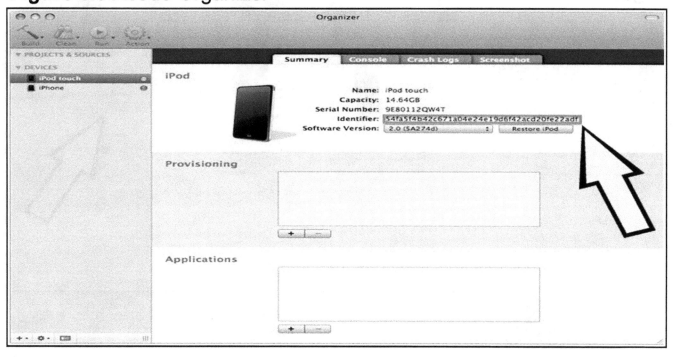

iTunes 7.7 Alternative

Another way to get your device ID, is to open iTunes 7.7 or later. By clicking on your device you will be able to see the number next to *Identifier*.

Figure 6.4 iTunes 7.7 Alternative

Fill In Info

Once you have your information filled in, click **Continue** and you will now have registered your device!

Figure 6.5 Fill In Info

App IDs

Short chapter, seems complicated but it's not.

Steps

7

Why Are We Doing This?

In this chapter we will discuss creating an App ID for you. Essentially, an App ID is a little identifier that distinguishes your app.

You will create a different App ID for every app you make. There is a generic App ID that Xcode already creates for you called *iOS Wildcard App ID*, that allows you to build and install multiple apps with a single ID (Called a suite of apps).

We'll use these later on in the chapter.

App IDs Section

From Certificates, Identifiers & Profiles, navigate your way to the Identifiers section, and click on App IDs. This is where you can create new App IDs and manage your existing IDs.

From this page, click on the **+** sign in the top right corner.

Figure 7.1 App IDs Section

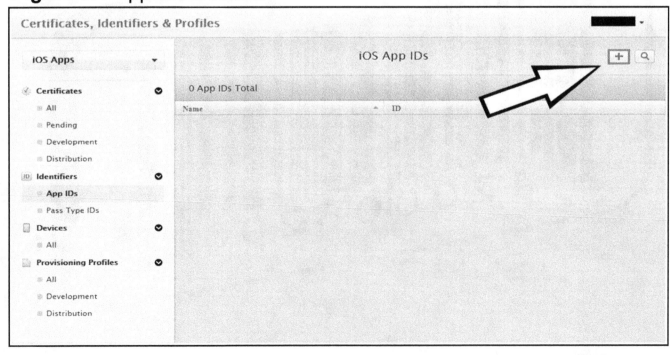

Create App ID

Here is where you will create your App ID. You only need to look at two things, this is how you should fill out those boxes:

App ID Description: Just put the name of your app.

App ID Suffix:

Explicit App ID: "com.MyCompany.MyApp"

Wildcard App ID: "com.MyCompany.*"

A Wildcard App ID will let you use the same ID for multiple apps, which means it doesn't pertain to any app in particular. As you can see above, *MyApp* was replaced with an asterisk (*). The asterisk is a placeholder for whatever the *Bundle Identifier* in Xcode is (The name of the particular app).

Click **Continue** at the bottom of the page.

Figure 7.2 Create App ID

Provisioning Profiles

These will allow you to utilize your devices.

Steps

So What Does This Mean?

1. Provisioning Section

2. Choose Profile Type

3. Creating A Non-App-Specific Profile

4. Creating An App-Specific Profile

5. Download Your Profiles

6. Apply Your Profiles

7. Success! The Profiles Are Now Active

8

So What Does This Mean?

To run your code on any device, you first must have a Provisioning Profile. There are two types of Provisioning Profiles, Development and Distribution. Development profiles allow you to test and run your app. Distribution profiles allow you to do the final run of your code and prepare it for sale. Distribution profiles can be made in one of two ways:

Non-app-specific: Usually used when making a suite of apps. It replaces the App ID with the generic one, and the name of it will be *YourCompany*.

App-Specific: More common, used when making an individual app with an App ID.

Provisioning Section

From Certificates, Identifiers & Profiles, navigate your way to the Provisioning Profiles section. Here you can create and manage different Provisioning Profiles.

To add a new profile, click the **+** sign in the top right corner of the page.

Figure 8.1 Provisioning Section

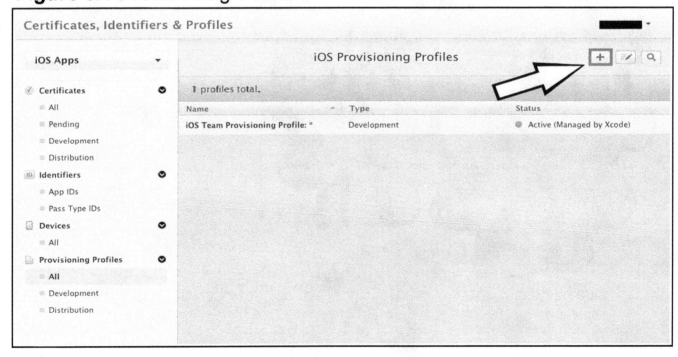

Choose Profile Type

Here, you can choose to make a development profile, or a distribution profile.

Development profiles are used for the basic running of your app on a device, and debugging it.

By default, Xcode creates a development profile for you, using the *iOS Wildcard App ID* we discussed earlier. That means that this profile is not specific to any app in particular, and may be used to run anything on your devices.

It is recommended that you keep this singular development profile, as it is unnecessary and confusing to make a different one for every App.

Distribution profiles will allow you to build your app for distribution (selling) on any of your devices. By default there are no existing profiles, so you will have to create one by selecting **App Store** under the *Distribution* heading.

Figure 8.2 Choose Profile Type

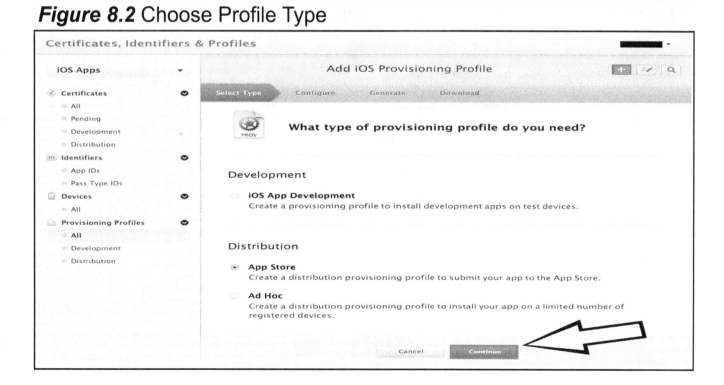

Creating A Non-App-Specific Profile

Read this page, and the next page before doing anything, to get insight on what's happening.

A Non-App-Specific Provisioning Profile let's you distribute your app under the general name of *YourCompany*, and does not pertain to any app in particular. Non-app-specific profiles use the iOS Wildcard App ID to make the profiles, because it is a generalized App ID as we have said earlier.

Fill out the boxes on the upcoming pages. In order:

App ID: Select the *iOS Wildcard App ID* option, assuming you have it.

Certificate: Your distribution certificate.

Profile Name: Your company's name.

Figure 8.3 Creating A Non-App-Specific Profile

Creating An App-Specific Profile

An App-Specific Provisioning Profile let's you distribute your app under the name of your app. It is recommended that you eventually make a profile for your company (non-specific), and one for your app (specific).

Fill out the boxes on the upcoming pages. In order:

App ID: Select your app's App ID.

Certificate: Your distribution certificate.

Profile Name: Your app's name.

Figure 8.4 Creating An App-Specific Profile

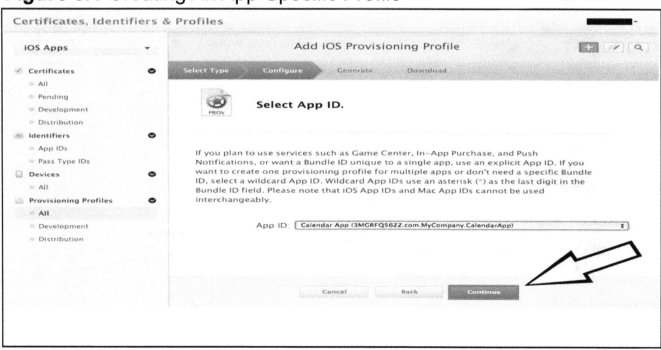

Download Your Profiles

Once you have finished creating both of you profiles, specific and non-specific, you must download them.

After you have made each profile, you should have gotten a screen like this one, just click the blue **Download** button in the centre of the page, and save your profile somewhere you won't forget it.

Figure 8.5 Download Your Profiles

Apply Your Profiles

When you have downloaded your profiles, select them and open them in Xcode.

Figure 8.6 Apply Your Profiles

Success! The Profiles Are Now Active

After you opened the profiles in Xcode, they should appear in the Provisioning Profiles section of your Organizer. They will be active and we can then use them in the next chapter!

Figure 8.7 Success! The Profiles Are Now Active

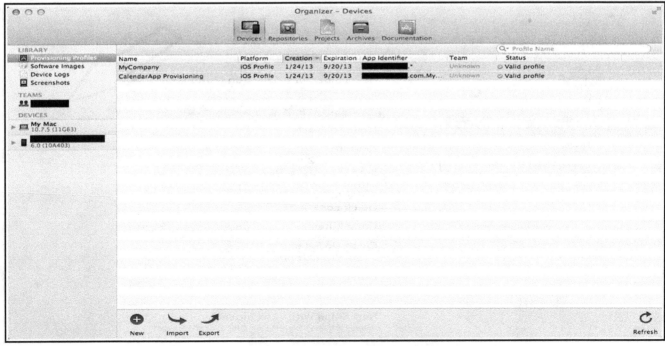

Getting Access To Contracts

**This is important!
Really!**

This Is Getting Serious, Man

In the last chapters, we finished getting all your "virtual certificates" and such. Now, in order to legally create anything for the App store, you have to fill in some forms.

Luckily, in this chapter you won't be filling out any forms. That's the next chapter. In this chapter you will be introduced to the world of iTunes Connect and where to find your forms.

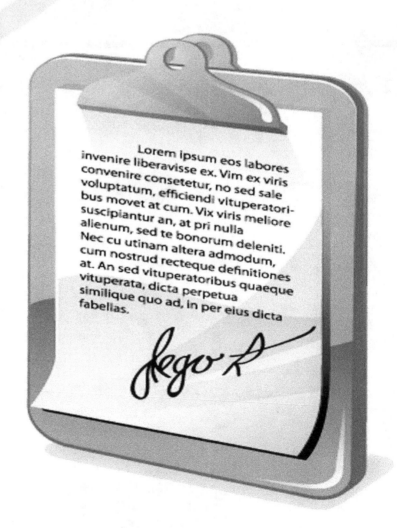

Log Into iTunes Connect

https://itunesconnect.apple.com/WebObjects/iTunesConnect.woa

Previously, we discussed the Certificates, Identifiers & Profiles site which is used for reference and signing certificates. Now, we will take a look at the ultimately more important **iTunes Connect**, which is used for submitting your app, keeping track of the money, and handling the banking.

Figure 9.1 Log Into iTunes Connect

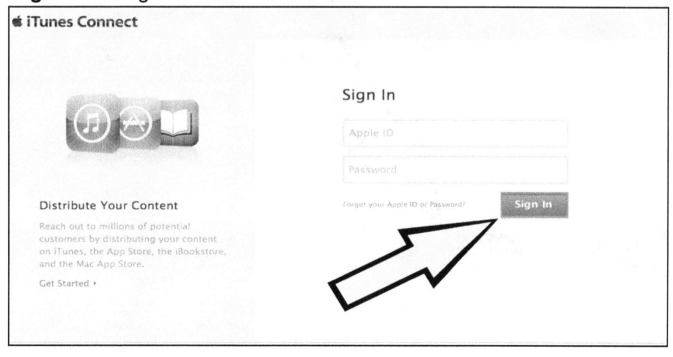

iTunes Connect Homepage

The iTunes Connect homepage gives you access to all the app managing things you need. From banking, to managing your apps and users, and even forums to help you, this site gives you all of those things. Right now, we will be looking at the **Contracts, Tax, and Banking** section.

Figure 9.2 iTunes Connect Homepage

information and iAdSuite sample codes, see the iOS Developer Library. If you want to join the iAd Network, go to developer.apple.com/iad.

iAd is a new mobile advertising platform that com[...] [...]e emotion of TV ads with the interactivity of the web. For an opportunity to earn advertising reve[...] [...]e iAd Network and enable ads in your applications. Learn more ⌐.

To use iAd in your applications, your Team[...] [...]t agree to the iAd Network Contract. Note that you must agree to the latest version of the iP[...] [...]per Program Agreement **before** you can access the iAd Network Contract.

Sales and Trends
Preview or download your daily [...]kly sales information here.

Manage Your Applications
Add, view, and manage your applications in the iTunes Store.

Contracts, Tax, and Banking
Manage your contracts, tax, and banking information.

Catalog Reports
Request catalog reports for your App Store content.

Payments and Financial Reports
View and download your monthly financial reports and payments.

Developer Forums
Find solutions and share tips with Apple developers from around the world.

Contracts, Tax, And Banking

Right here, you will see three possible contracts that you have access to.

iOS Free Applications is already in effect and grants you full access to create as many free apps as you would like.

iOS Paid Applications must be filled out and requested. It allows you to actually *sell* an app on the App store.

iAd Network must be filled out and requested if you so choose. It allows your app to gain revenue from ads placed on it. It is completely optional, and not necessary whatsoever for publishing an app.

Figure 9.3 Contracts, Tax, And Banking

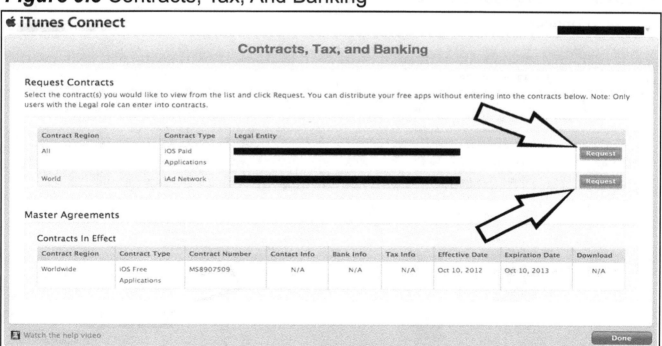

Request Your Contracts

From the previous page, click the **Request** button next to the contract you would like to receive. You will be prompted to agree to a Review Agreement. This agreement lets Apple know that you would like to sell your app through them, and receive a contract allowing such a thing to happen.

Figure 9.4 Request Your Contracts

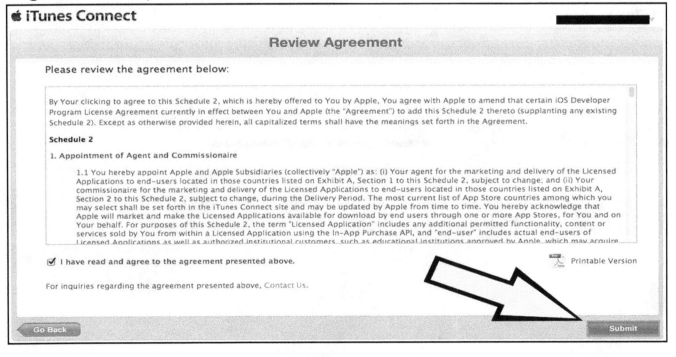

Yay! You Now Have Access To Legal Documents

Now that you have agreed to that little prompt, you will be emailed a copy of it. But the fun doesn't stop there, you can now go back to the Contracts, Tax, and Banking section, and fill out your banking information, as well as print out and mail the required contracts!

Figure 9.5 Thank You Page

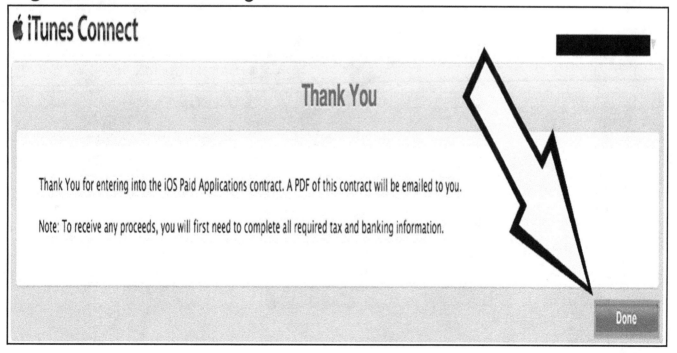

Filling Out Your Information

You gotta do this.
It's like necessary.

10

This Is Real World Stuff

Now that Apple finally gave you access to your forms. You can start filling them out. But first you might have some questions.

Why do they need these forms?

First off, they need to make sure of your:

• Identity - where you live, etc.

• Are you selling the app as an individual or a company?

Second thing they need is literally just how to pay you. iTunes deposits your profits *directly* into your bank account.

• Who is your bank?

• What is your bank account number?

Thirdly, they need to do this all legally, and with accordance to the tax laws of your country.

• Social insurance number?

• GST or other business tax number?

Most app creators fail at this point because it seems too complicated, but just methodically going through all the papers and filling in all the information will carry you to the other side.

Now To Set Up Your Info...

You now have access to the wonderful world of setting up your various information.

Contact Info is where you enter the contact information of all the people making your App.

Banking Info is all the information related to your bank account.

Tax Info are the physical forms that must be printed out, written on, and then mailed to Apple.

Figure 10.1 Contracts, Tax, and Banking

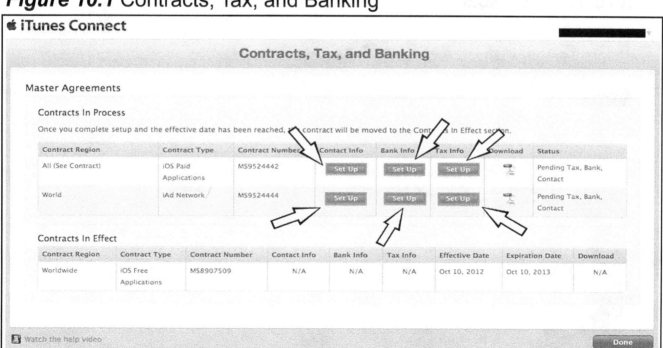

Setting Up Contacts

In this section, you are keeping track of who has what role in your "company". Simply click **Add New Contact,** fill out the appropriate information, and then next to each **Role** in the section below, select the appropriate contact you made.

When making the contact, you may notice the confusing word of **Title**. In that box, just fill out the role the person has at your company. For example, *President, Owner, Lead Programmer, Accountant, etc.*

If you are applying as an individual, you can just call yourself the Owner, and assign yourself to every role: Senior Management, Technical, Financial, etc.

Figure 10.2 Contacts

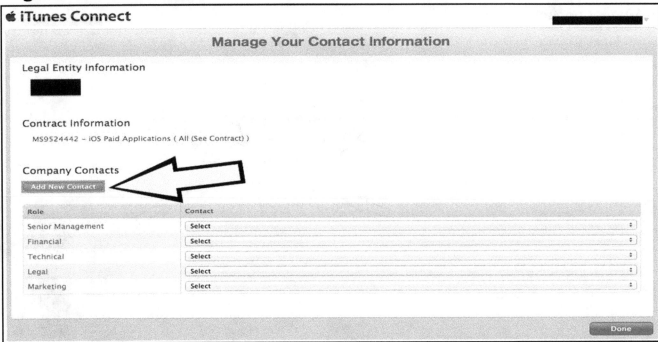

Setting Up Bank Info

In this next section, you will have to fill out some of your banking information. It's fairly straightforward, but you might not know what some things are.

TRANSIT Number is a way of routing payment to the proper bank.

SWIFT Number identifies your bank and branch.

ACCOUNT Number identifies your specific account in that bank's branch.

All of these things are needed for Apple to put money into your bank account. These pieces of information can be found at the bottom of your cheque, but it's best to get this information from your bank teller.

Figure 10.3 Banking Information

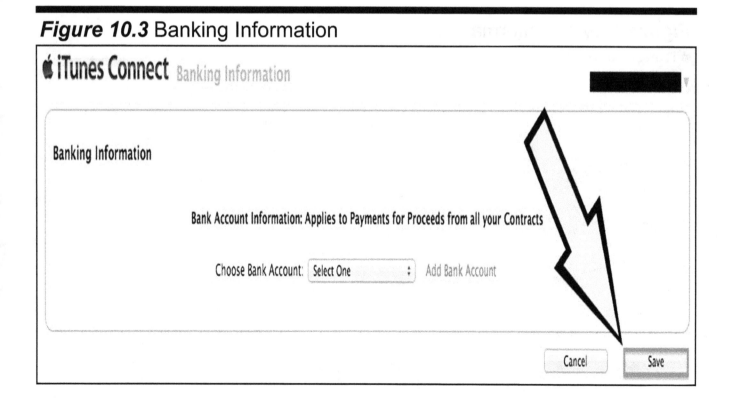

Setting Up Tax Info

This section deals with tax information. This tax information allows Apple to do business with you in accordance with the tax laws of each country.

The U.S. form in the picture must be completed regardless of where you are, whereas the Canadian and Australian form must only be filled out if you are in that country.

Figure 10.4 Tax Information

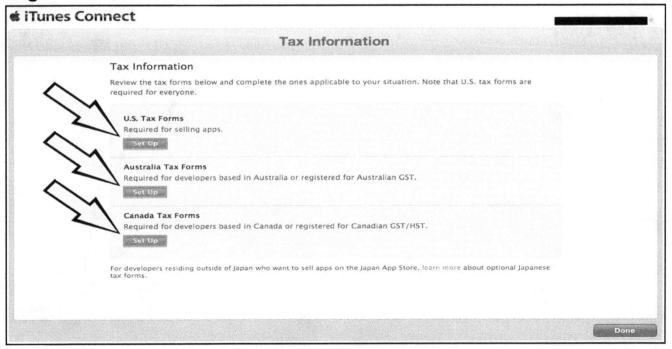

U.S. Tax Forms

If you are an American citizen, you will find yourself at this page. It simply asks if you are an individual or a business, and your TIN number (Tax Identification and Certification Number).

Simply, if you are an individual, it's your social security number (SSN); and if you are a business, it's your employee identification number (EIN).

If you are not a U.S. Citizen, you must apply for an EIN number. Thankfully, this is quite simple. Go to the following IRS web page, and follow the instructions. You can apply by phone or online, and after answering some questions you will receive your EIN number immediately. (They will also send a letter confirming your EIN number).

http://www.irs.gov/Businesses/Small-Businesses-&-Self-Employed/How-to-Apply-for-an-EIN

Figure 10.5 U.S. Tax Forms

Tax Information

Once you submit this form, you will not be able to make changes via iTunes Connect. Please make sure this information is correct before you click Submit.

Download Form W-9 Instructions

Form W-9: Request for Taxpayer Identification Number and Certification

(Rev. December 2011)

1. Name:
(as shown on your income tax return)

2. Business Name:
(If different from above)

3. Type of Beneficial Owner: Other (see instructions)

4. Exempt Payee: ◯   Subject to Backup Withholding: ◯

5. Address: Select One   Add Address

Requester's name and address: Apple Inc.
1 Infinite Loop
Cupertino, CA 95014

Canadian And Other Country Tax Forms

The Canadian tax form can be somewhat confusing with terminology, but simply, unless you are electing someone to represent you, just fill out parts A and D of the form. If you have a GST number, be sure to include that. It is important that you fill this form in, sign it, and then mail it to the address provided on the form. If you are a Quebec citizen, there is a separate form for you.

Our advice to everyone, would be to courier (FedEx, UPS, etc) this form to insure that it arrives safely. It costs a little more, but it is worth the investment, as you will get confirmation of delivery.

Figure 10.6 Canadian Tax Forms

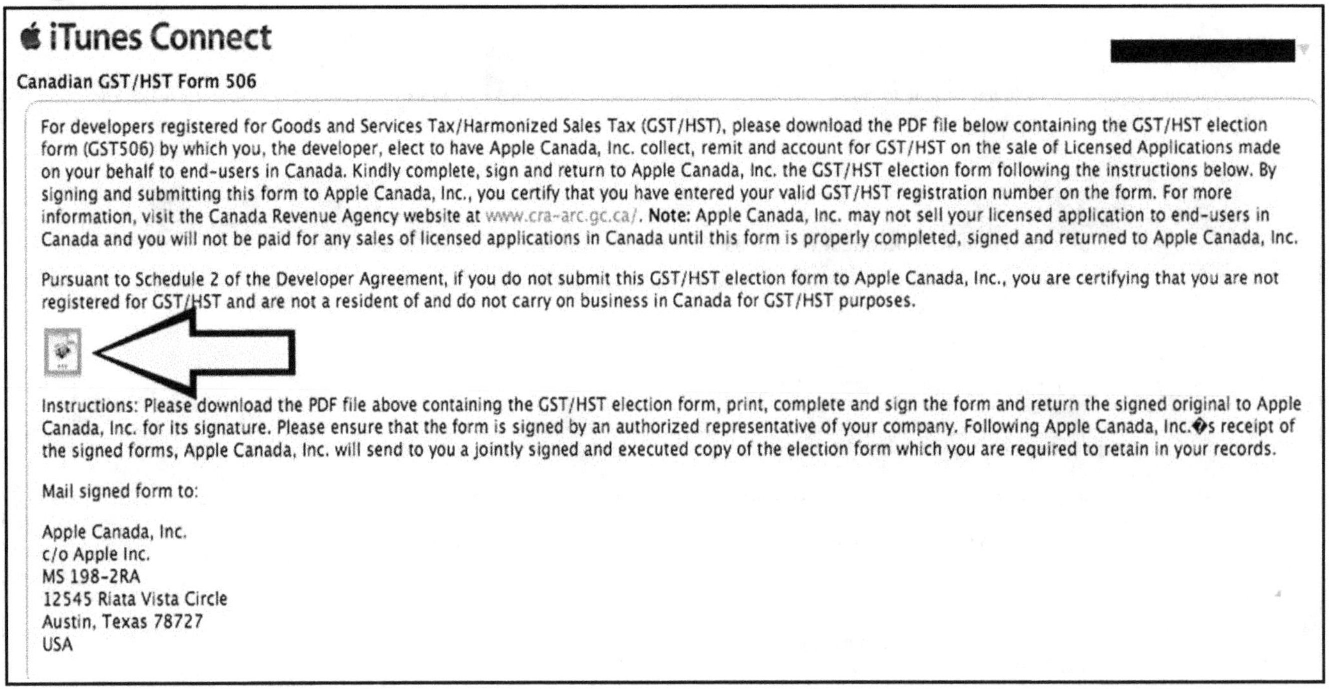

iTunes Connect [redacted]

Canadian GST/HST Form 506

For developers registered for Goods and Services Tax/Harmonized Sales Tax (GST/HST), please download the PDF file below containing the GST/HST election form (GST506) by which you, the developer, elect to have Apple Canada, Inc. collect, remit and account for GST/HST on the sale of Licensed Applications made on your behalf to end-users in Canada. Kindly complete, sign and return to Apple Canada, Inc. the GST/HST election form following the instructions below. By signing and submitting this form to Apple Canada, Inc., you certify that you have entered your valid GST/HST registration number on the form. For more information, visit the Canada Revenue Agency website at www.cra-arc.gc.ca/. **Note:** Apple Canada, Inc. may not sell your licensed application to end-users in Canada and you will not be paid for any sales of licensed applications in Canada until this form is properly completed, signed and returned to Apple Canada, Inc.

Pursuant to Schedule 2 of the Developer Agreement, if you do not submit this GST/HST election form to Apple Canada, Inc., you are certifying that you are not registered for GST/HST and are not a resident of and do not carry on business in Canada for GST/HST purposes.

Instructions: Please download the PDF file above containing the GST/HST election form, print, complete and sign the form and return the signed original to Apple Canada, Inc. for its signature. Please ensure that the form is signed by an authorized representative of your company. Following Apple Canada, Inc.�s receipt of the signed forms, Apple Canada, Inc. will send to you a jointly signed and executed copy of the election form which you are required to retain in your records.

Mail signed form to:

Apple Canada, Inc.
c/o Apple Inc.
MS 198-2RA
12545 Riata Vista Circle
Austin, Texas 78727
USA

And Now You Wait...

Now that you have filled out all the required information, and mailed the required forms, it will take some time for this all to take effect. It generally takes 3-12 weeks for Apple to process your forms. For some reason, individuals , rather than companies, seem to get processed faster. The ONLY way you will know whether you have been processed, is by checking your iTunes Connect account, and looking at the Contacts, Tax and Banking section. Unless your page looks like the picture you see, with effective and expiration dates, it has not been processed yet.

Figure 10.7 Completed Contracts

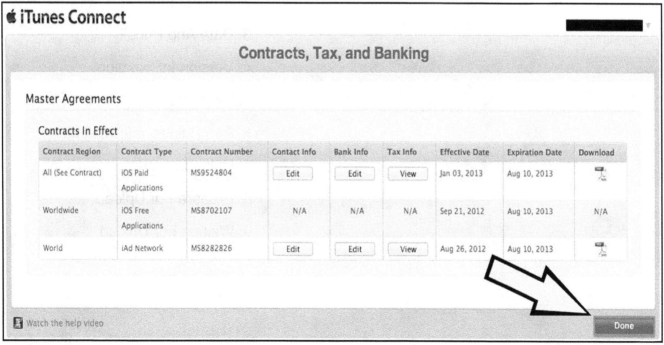

 iTunes Connect

Contracts, Tax, and Banking

Master Agreements

Contracts In Effect

Contract Region	Contract Type	Contract Number	Contact Info	Bank Info	Tax Info	Effective Date	Expiration Date	Download
All (See Contract)	iOS Paid Applications	MS9524804	Edit	Edit	View	Jan 03, 2013	Aug 10, 2013	
Worldwide	iOS Free Applications	MS8702107	N/A	N/A	N/A	Sep 21, 2012	Aug 10, 2013	N/A
World	iAd Network	MS8282826	Edit	Edit	View	Aug 26, 2012	Aug 10, 2013	

 Watch the help video

Done

Adding A New App

This is almost it! Your App is being made a reality.

Steps

We're Getting Close!

1. Manage Your Apps

2. App Information

3. Date And Price

4. Version Information

5. Metadata

6. App Review Information

7. Uploads

8. Prepare For Upload

9. Waiting For Upload

We're Getting Close!

In this chapter, we'll be putting your app's information on the iTunes Connect site. This will include everything that the Apple Review Team will need to decide whether to approve or decline your app.

Manage Your Apps

From the iTunes Connect homepage, click on **Manage Your Applications**. From this page, you will be able to see and manage all the apps you make in the future. Right now, we will be adding your app on here. First, start by clicking the blue **Add New App** button.

Figure 11.1 Manage Your Apps

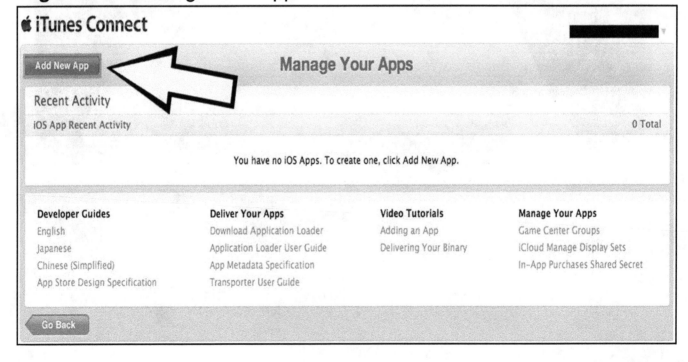

App Information

Here, you will enter some basic information about your app. In case you don't know, here's how to fill it out:

Default Language: English.

App Name: The name of your app as you want it to appear in the App Store, ex: *CalendarApp*

SKU Number: A simple code to distinguish your app. The syntax that we used in the picture is fairly straightforward. MC stands for *MyCompany*. CA stands for *CalendarApp*. 001 stands for the fact that it is our *first* app. You don't have to use this syntax, but it's easier.

Bundle ID: You will select your App ID.

Figure 11.2 App Information

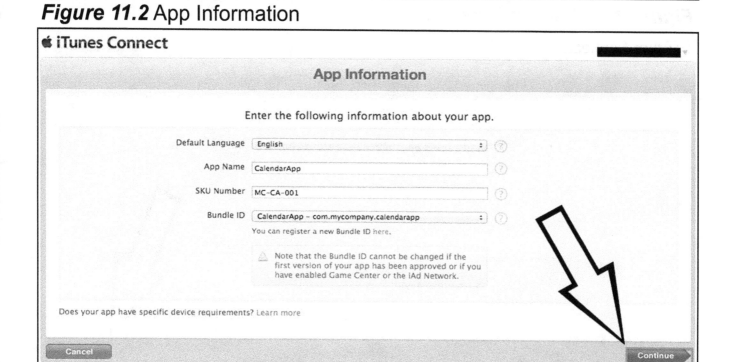

Date And Price

In this section, we are going to set the date and price for our app. Generally, unless you want to have a specific release date, you can just leave it as the current date. Underneath, you can set your app's price tier. There are 87 price tiers, ranging from $0.99 to $999.99. Tier one is the cheapest at $0.99, so we will pick that for our example.

At the bottom of the page there are two check boxes. Unless you want your app to be free to schools, or only available to volume purchase customers, you should leave those blank.

Figure 11.3 Date And Price

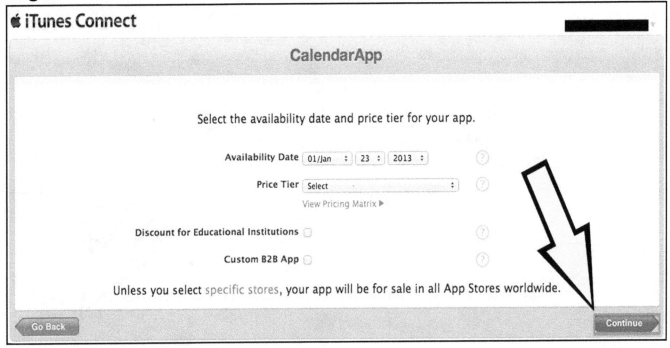

Version Information

Version Information will let Apple know what your app is about. If your app contains multiple occurrences of adult material, they will rate your app for an older age group, or may not even sell it.

Next to **Version Number**, fill in what version your app is. Normally, just put *1.0*, but say if you're releasing an update, then you would put *1.1* or *2.0*.

Next to **Copyright**, fill in the name of your company, preceded by the year you got rights to this App. ex: *2013 MyCompany*.

In **Categories**, select what genres your app falls into. ex: *Gaming, Business, etc.*

Figure 11.4 Version Information

 iTunes Connect

CalendarApp

Enter the following information in **English**.

Version Information

Version Number	1.0
Copyright	2013 MyCompany
Primary Category	Utilities
Secondary Category (Optional)	Productivity

Metadata

Metadata is all the information that customers will read, when they look at your App.

Description: This is a catchy synopsis of your app that people will read, and decide whether to buy your app. Make it simple, and able to get the point across easily.

Keywords: These are specific words that, when people search them, will turn up your app. You can have as many keywords as you want, but they will be less effective. Stick to a select few, that will always get your app.

Support URL: This is a website that you must have. It should contain support information on it so people can contact you.

Figure 11.5 Metadata

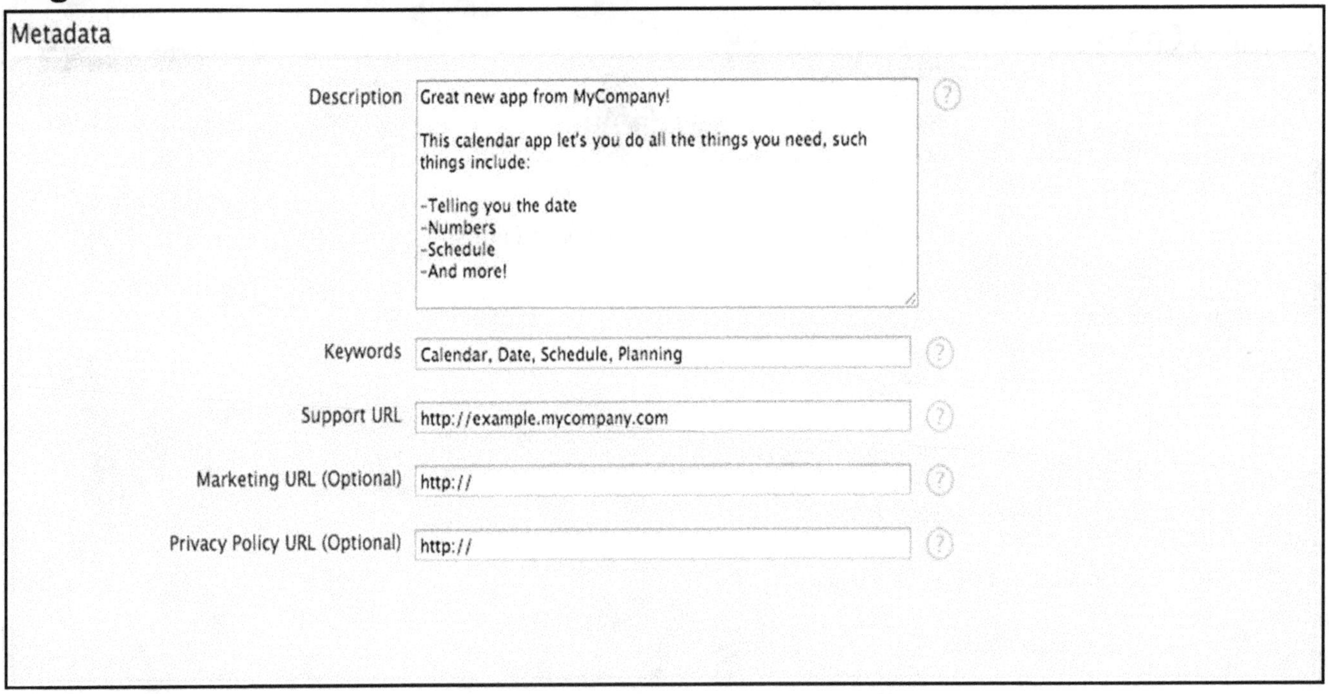

Metadata

Description: Great new app from MyCompany!

This calendar app let's you do all the things you need, such things include:

-Telling you the date
-Numbers
-Schedule
-And more!

Keywords: Calendar, Date, Schedule, Planning

Support URL: http://example.mycompany.com

Marketing URL (Optional): http://

Privacy Policy URL (Optional): http://

App Review Information

App Review Information is everything that the Apple review team needs to approve your app.

Contact Information: Just fill out your name, email, and phone number by which Apple can contact you if there is a problem.

Review Notes: This is where you put any additional information that you feel the Apple Review team should be aware of.

Demo Account Information: This is if you want to give the review team a password for your app. It must be mentioned in review notes as well.

Figure 11.6 App Review Information

App Review Information

   Contact Information (?)

First Name	John
Last Name	Smith
Email Address	JohnSmith@example.com
Phone Number	1-555-123-4567
	Include your country code

Review Notes (Optional) (?)

Demo Account Information (Optional) (?)

Username	
Password	

Uploads

Uploads are the screenshots of your app that people will see. Try to have as many screenshots as you can, as it will advertise your app better. Just to clarify:

Large App Icon: This is a 1024x1024 square icon for your app on the App Store.

3.5-Inch Retina Display Screenshots: These are screen shots of your app taken on the 3.5-inch retina display, i.e. Anything before the iPhone 5.

4-Inch Retina Display Screenshots: These are screenshots taken of your app on the 4-inch retina display, i.e. iPhone 5.

Figure 11.7 Uploads

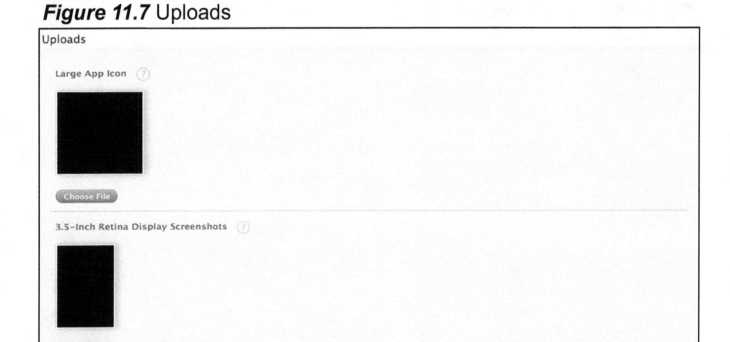

Prepare For Upload

Now that you finished filling out the info for your app, it should be viewable in the **Manage Your Applications** section of iTunes Connect.

Right away this screen should pop up. If you'll notice, under the current version of your app, it'll say **Prepare for Upload**.

What you need to do is click the **View Details** button at the bottom, and then proceed to click the blue **Upload Binary** button that will appear in the top right hand corner.

Figure 11.8 Prepare For Upload

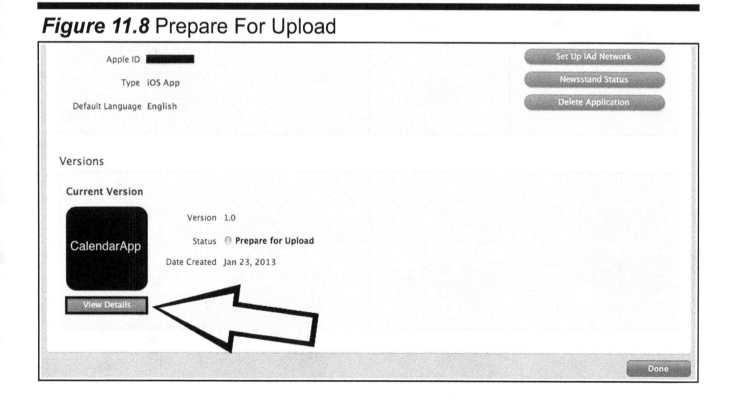

Waiting For Upload

Once you reach this step, your app "binary" is ready for upload. An app binary is a file that Xcode can export, that essentially contains your app. You have to upload this file, and then the Apple review team will look over it.

We will do that in the next chapter.

Figure 11.9 Waiting For Upload

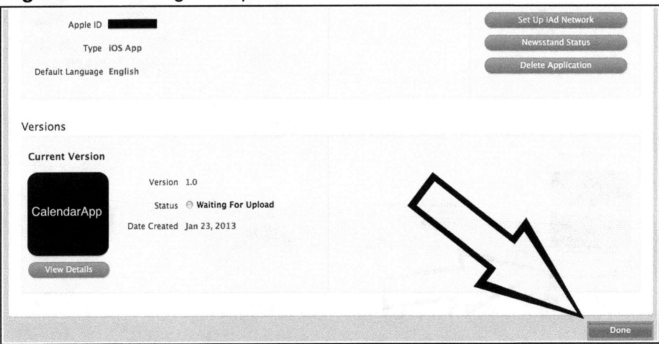

Preparing App
For Archiving

It's practically done! We just have to prep our App.

Steps

Just Changing Settings...

12

Just Changing Settings...

Chapter's 12 and 13 follow the steps required to prep and submit your app to the App store through Xcode. These chapters will only apply to some people.

So, here's where we're at. You're either making or buying an app.

If you're making an app, like with code and stuff, you will need to do the stuff in this chapter. (If you have already done these things, it can't hurt to look them over again and double check).

If you are buying an app, say, from some guy, he will either have done one of two things:

• He already did the things in this chapter and gave you the **App Binary** file.

• He gave you an Xcode file with a bunch of code and stuff in it.

If he gave you an App Binary file (He would know what that is) then you can completely avoid Chapters 12 and 13, and submit your app directly to the App store using Apple's **Application Loader**.

The Application Loader is an application built into Xcode. (It looks just like that big blue image on this page). You don't have to open Xcode to use it, just right click on the Xcode application and select **Show Package Contents**. From there just go to:

Contents > Applications > Application Loader

Once in the Application Loader, you can deliver your app using the App Binary file you have. Now you're done. Just wait for approval on iTunes connect.

If, however, the guy just gave you an Xcode file with a bunch of code written in it, then you will most likely have to follow the instructions in Chapters 12 and 13. (If he didn't do that already himself).

Apple's Application Loader Icon

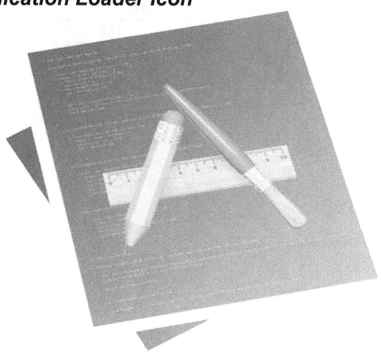

Duplicate "Release" Configuration

This step will copy your app's release configuration. A release configuration is a series of settings that configure your app for *Release* (using the app), as opposed to *Debugging* (testing the app).

First, open Xcode, and start by going to the location in the picture:

CalendarApp > Project > CalendarApp > Info

Then, under **Configurations**, click the **+** button. You will get a drop down menu, and from there, click **Duplicate "Release" Configuration**.

This should create a new configuration directly underneath the release one.

Figure 12.1 Duplicate "Release" Configuration

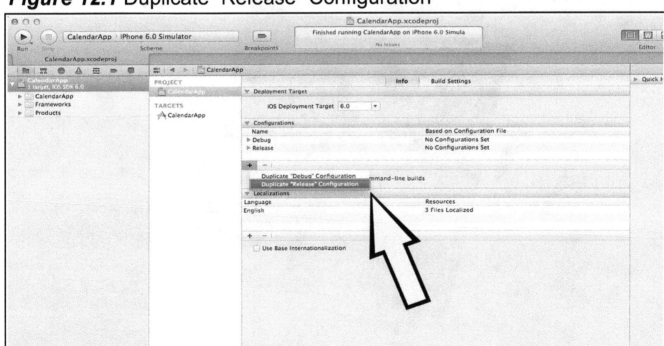

Rename "Release" Configuration Copy

We will be renaming the copy of the release configuration from "Release" to "Distribution". This will effectively create a new configuration called *Distribution* (selling your app), which we will modify in the next steps.

Double click on the name of the release configuration copy, and rename it to "Distribution".

Figure 12.2 Rename "Release" Configuration Copy

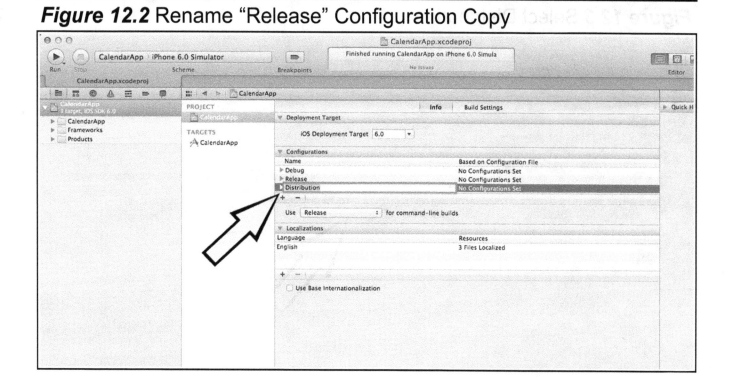

Select Distribution

Here we are selecting the distribution configuration to be used.

Underneath the **+** sign, where it says **Use Release for command-line builds**, change *Release* to *Distribution* in the drop down menu.

Figure 12.3 Select Distribution

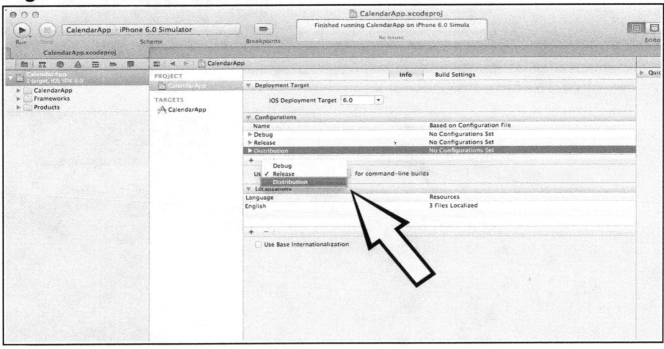

Change Distribution Code Signing

In this step, we will be changing the code signing for the distribution configuration to the app-specific Provisioning Profile we created earlier. it should be labelled as "CalendarApp Provisioning" or something along those lines.

Navigate to the location in the picture by simply clicking **Build Settings** instead of **Info** as we did on page 92. Then, scroll down to the **Code Signing** section and select "CalendarApp Provisioning" in the green drop down menu next to **Distribution**.

CalendarApp > Project > CalendarApp > Build Settings > Code Signing > Distribution > "CalendarApp Provisioning"

Figure 12.4 Change Distribution Code Signing

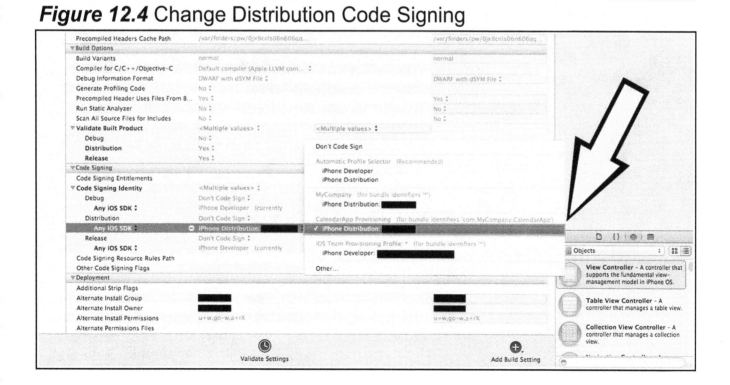

Rename Bundle Identifier

Now, we are going to rename your app's *bundle identifier* from it's current name as "com.MyCompany.${PRODUCT_NAME}", to "com.MyCompany.CalendarApp".

${PRODUCT_NAME} is a placeholder for whatever the name of your App is. As your app name may be different from your bundle identifier, it would cause trouble if you didn't change it.

First, you need to find your app's Info.plist file. it is usually located at:

CalendarApp > Supporting Files > CalendarApp-Info.plist

Find the **Bundle Identifier** key, and change it to your actual bundle identifier.

Figure 12.5 Rename Bundle Identifier

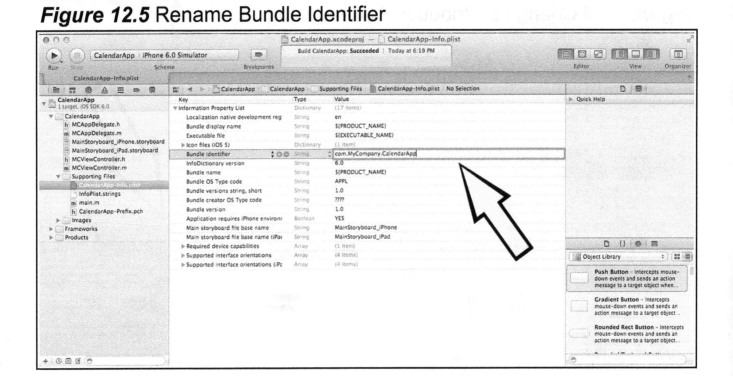

See Updated Bundle Identifier

Assuming you did the previous step correctly, the new and correct bundle identifier should now appear in clear writing as shown below.

CalendarApp > Targets > CalendarApp > Summary

At the top, next to Bundle Identifier should be the new one you just entered.

Figure 12.6 See Updated Bundle Identifier

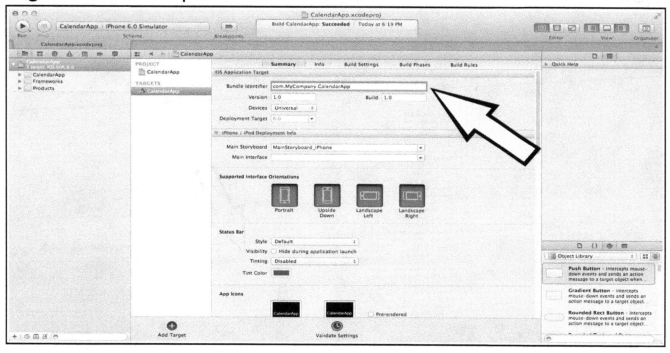

Change App Name

Here is where you can change or modify the name of your app. You can modify this text box, and whatever name you put in it will be the name as people see it on the App Store.

CalendarApp > Targets > CalendarApp > Build Settings > Packaging > Product Name

Then change the name of your app as you see fit.

Figure 12.7 Change App Name

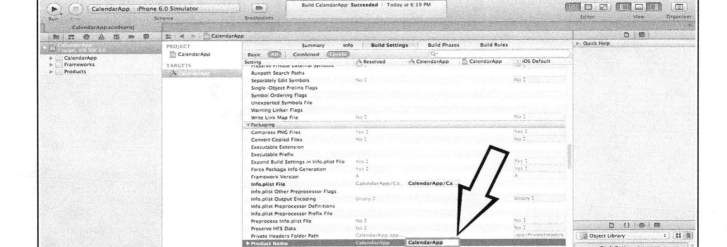

Edit Scheme

Now, we are going to edit the scheme of your app. This will essentially tell Xcode which configuration to run, as well as where to run it.

In Xcode still, next to the **Stop** button in the top left corner, click on the name of your app. From the drop down menu, click the **Edit Scheme** button.

Figure 12.8 Edit Scheme

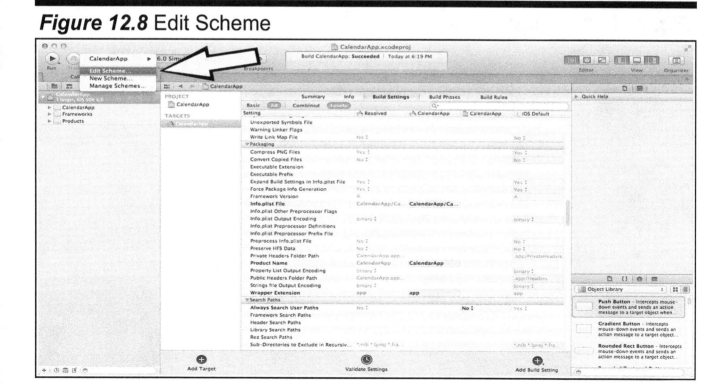

Change Destination

In the **Archiving** section of this new menu, at the top of the page, change **Destination** to *iOS Device* or whatever iOS device you have plugged in.

This will eventually make your app be run through your iOS device.

Figure 12.9 Change Destination

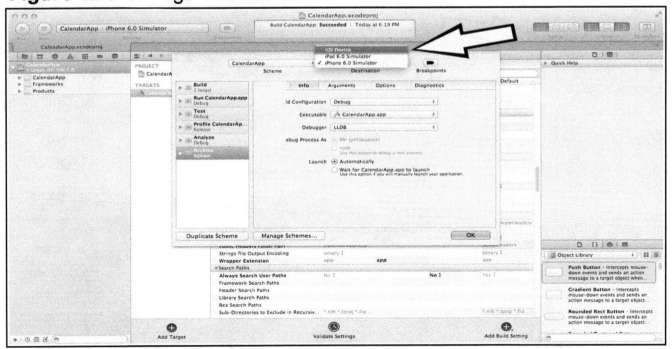

Change Build Configuration

You are now going to have to change the current build configuration for **Archiving** from *Release* to *Distribution*. This will make your app run the distribution configuration, and then prepare it for sale.

From the current menu:

Archiving > Build Configuration

In the drop down menu, change the current selection to *Distribution*.

Figure 12.10 Change Build Configuration

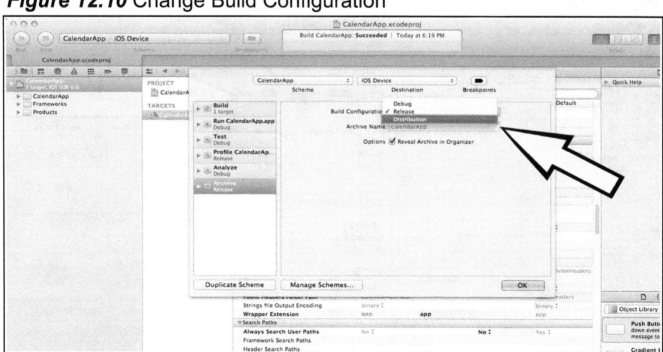

Archive App

Now we are going to build your app for **Archiving**. This will run your app through your iOS device, and prepare it for selling. Once your app has run, It will appear in the Xcode Organizer under the **Archives** tab.

From the toolbar at the top of the page:

Product > Archive

OR

Product > Build For > Archiving

Figure 12.11 Archive App

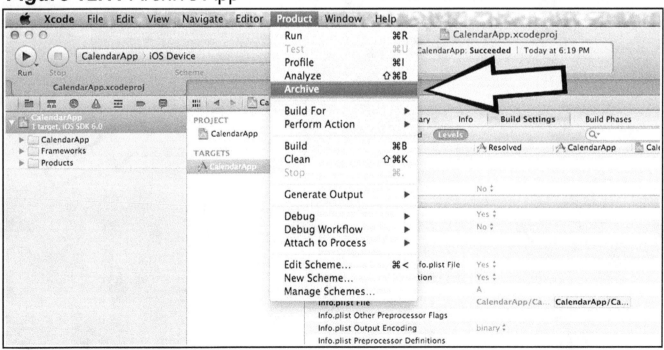

Submit To App Store

This is it! The final steps! Hooray!

13

Success! You Made It!

Now, your app should be finished. You have archived it, and it is now resting in the Xcode Organizer waiting to be submitted to the App Store. In this chapter we are going to submit your app to the App Store.

Validate App

From the Xcode Organizer, go to the **Archives** tab at the top of the page. Here you can view all your archived apps. Right now we are going to validate your app, which means Xcode will quickly check it over and make sure it's not wrong somewhere.

Click the **Validate** button on the right hand side of the organizer.

Figure 13.1 Validate App

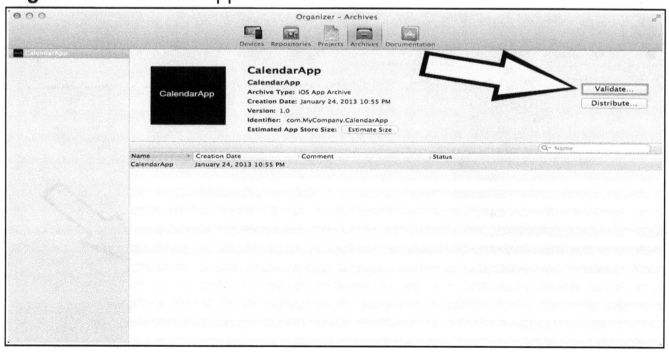

Log Into iTunes Connect

Simply log into iTunes connect so Xcode knows where to find your App ID, etc.

Then click **Next**.

Figure 13.2 Log Into iTunes Connect

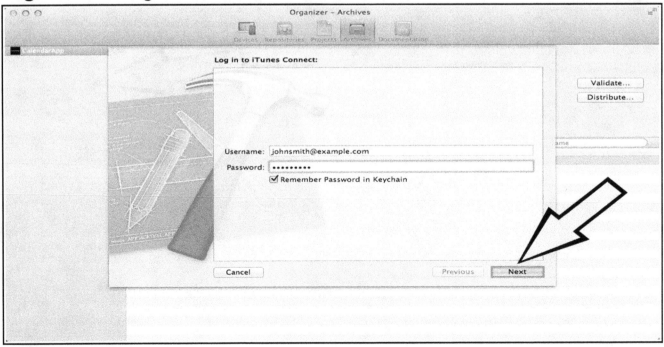

Application And Identity

Here we are going to select which app you are submitting, as well as who is responsible for the code signing of this app.

Next to **Application** select the app you are submitting.

Next to **Code Signing Identity** select your name or whoever is code signing the app.

Then click **Next**.

Figure 13.3 Application And Identity

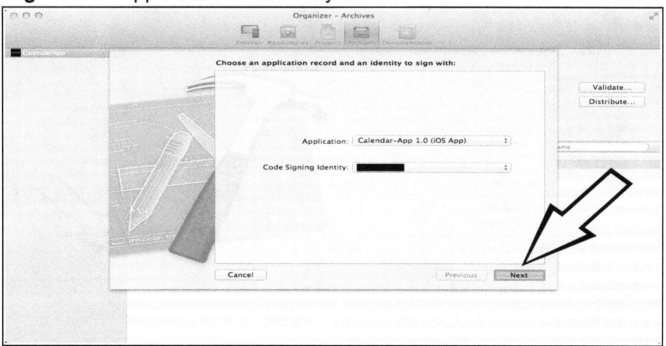

Validation Succeeded

If Xcode found no problems with your app, it should say **Validation Succeeded**. If not, then go back into the code, and change whatever is wrong. You can then simply archive the app again and retry validating it.

Click **Finish**.

Figure 13.4 Validation Succeeded

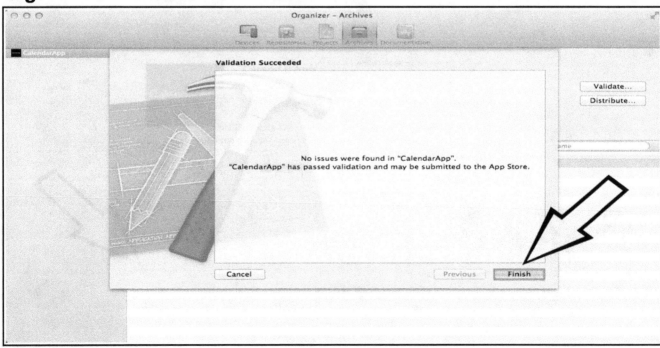

Distribute App

From the Xcode Organizer again, click the **Distribute** button underneath the **Validate** button. We will be finally submitting your app to the App Store.

Now, you will have to select the method of distribution.

Submit to the iOS App Store: This is the conventional method as it will put your app directly on the App Store. (Click this).

Save for Enterprise or Ad-Hoc Deployment: This will let you sell the app outside of the App Store. Don't worry about it.

Export as Xcode Archive: This allows you to create an archived file of your app to give or sell for later submission.

Figure 13.5 Distribute App

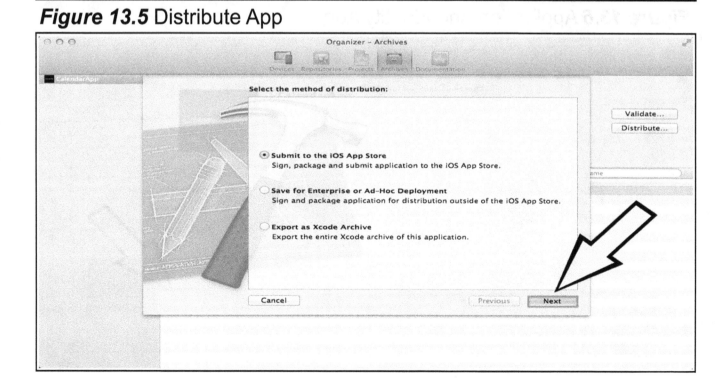

Application And Identity Again

We are going to choose which app and who code signed it as we did earlier.

Application: Choose your app.

Code Signing Identity: Your name, or whoever code signed the app.

Figure 13.6 Application And Identity Again

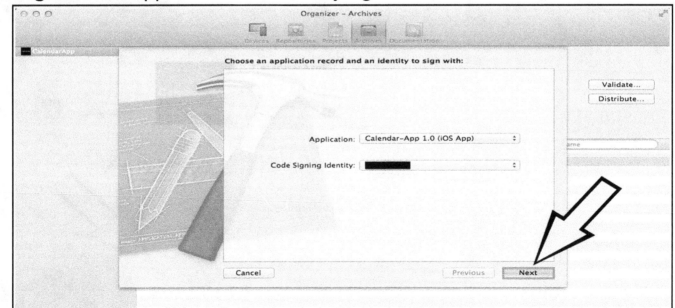

Submission Succeeded

If nothing went wrong, it should say **Submission Succeeded**. Your app should have been submitted to the app Store for a review team to look at it.

Figure 13.7 Submission Succeeded

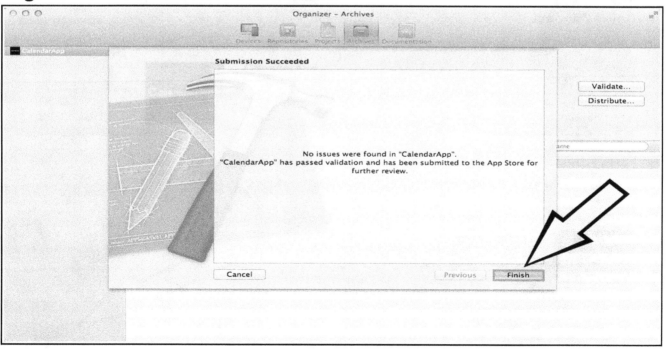

App Status Waiting For Review

Your app's status in iTunes Connect should now be changed to **Waiting For Review**. There are a total of 18 different app statuses that your app can be in, ranging from incomplete contracts, to rejected by the review team. If you are ever curious about what a status means, you can find that in the Developer Library.

If all went as planned, your app should be approved and up on the App Store. As always, you can view your app in iTunes Connect.

Figure 13.8 App Status Waiting For Review

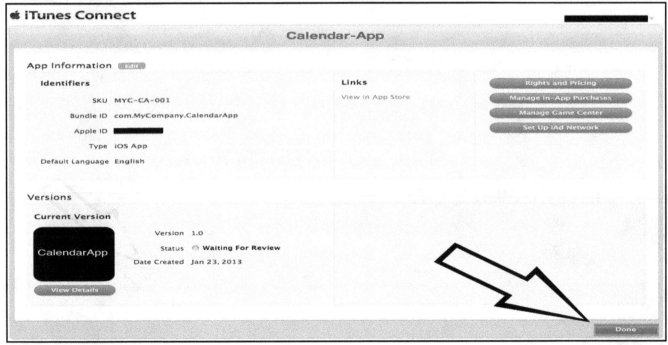

Thank You

Thank you for purchasing and reading this book.

If you have any suggestions, or would like to be updated on our latest books, you can send an email to:

grantworksmedia@gmail.com